AUTOBIOGRAPHY OF ENVELOPES

BURNING DECK

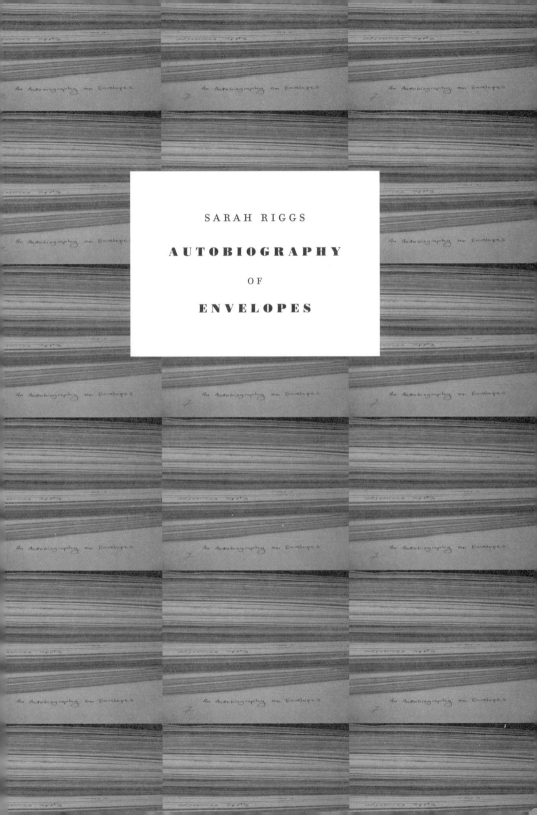

SARAH RIGGS

AUTOBIOGRAPHY

OF

ENVELOPES

Burning Deck is the literature program of
Anyart: Contemporary Arts Center,
a tax exempt (501c3), non-profit corporation.

Designed by Quemadura
Photographs by Marie Borel

ISBN 978-1-936194-10-0
(original paperback)

DISTRIBUTORS:

Small Press Distribution
1341 Seventh St., Berkeley, CA 94710
www.spdbooks.org, 800-869-7553

Spectacular Diseases
c/o Paul Green, 83b London Rd.
Peterborough, Cambs. PE2 9BS, UK

FOR PETER GIZZI

We make out of the quarrel with others, rhetoric, but of the quarrel with ourselves, poetry.

> I call to the mysterious one who yet
> Shall walk the wet sands by the edge of the stream
> And look most like me, being indeed my double,
> And prove of all imaginable things
> The most unlike, being my anti-self,
> And standing by these characters, disclose
> All that I seek; and whisper it as though
> He were afraid the birds, who cry aloud
> Their momentary cries before its dawn
> Would carry it away . . .

WILLIAM BUTLER YEATS, "Per Amica Silentia Lunae"

A

A bird, a spider, some children's
cries were present. I heard the
hour, it was one. The president
was shot years before. Someone
was born, just when I began to breathe.

(Inside the envelope are scraps).

The plants and lives of other animals
would come to be. They and the jumble
would be one. It turns and turns. We can
regard it as loss. (Sometimes we—can't
help but—feel it as loss).

And other elements of a trickle
or tendency, but to tell tales
& in other ways hold a ring, thought,
and phone in one hand: while
saying I'll be there & eating an apricot.

I heard it on the radio, this false
sense of security—we all did,
and in the wind. We can't write
each other letters because contacting
a surface is self-conscious. How
random is the iris that grows
where it is planted.

Out of nature, out of time, out of
everything. The apocalyptic thinking
of the nature of the metaphor. We are
in time at present. Do we drop
out when we die? The spider is neither
content nor discontent in its web. The
rain asunders in.

Changeling featured in grass alcove
hollows. The world receives its bidding.
We thought we knew where we were.
Every hour. The impression of moving
forward, yet with each step we get closer
to what's too near.

When she removed the patch, his
hallucinations fluttered in the opening,
brain, heart—he was dying. Shared
distortion. Remain hours, minutes,
seconds, until they no longer remain:
for that person.

A rain, a twirl of hour, we are recomposed.
Lightening falls in a jagged sort of way.
I can't remember myself but for the brambles,
the price tags, and reindeers. Mon cher
we are together. Can you remain? These
resemblances of hours may not be enough.

If we open the envelope there may be
nothing inside. Is it our job to fill it? With what
body or idea? And will you explain the
difference. The random way we receive cat calls
and missives. The hour wrenches open, there
were five animals who came to inhabit it.

Mellifluous, guttural chatter. The training is
so to speak good. Lastly the hour opens out either
upwards or downwards, depending on this place.
A casting of the die, a trumpeting of appeals,
a merited sensation. Quick, here it comes again:
a band of light.

Hopefully what was inside the envelopes
was not also outside. A melon cannot fit in there
for instance. We open it and remove the seeds.
And so: the cats climb *along*. Difficult for a dog
to know how to do this. Rightfully so the tremendous
place beyond. Thought. I have ceased to want
to go there. I would like to remember I am here.

B

The rush hour was one of us or something.
Landing was the way of remaining here.
Tempted by the rain. And a variety
of fountains. This or that, this that.

My father wrote to me to suggest removing
the word "hopefully." He is certain. It
makes me unsure that the inside and
outside of the envelope are not one.

Here at the Café de la Poste
Pierre Joris & Michel Deguy (was it?)
were having a coffee together. And I was
here. And I am here. I have a ring with
a white band and four mini diamonds.
I am in the middle of me.

The rest of the hour is one. In this dark
band we call winter, there is not pearl
or mother of pearl, but white resin.
We rest in its seconds. Largely the hour
swallows us in. Lately the wedding glass
is just enough to drink from. Champagne.

The waitings & envelopes. The Suez Canal,
the Lazy Susan. The women waiting. Lehman
Brothers. A long lost friend. Wading in the
midst of it. Riding. Writing. Waiting into
the sense of self, it was I who found
the key, and I who use it.

A wash, a wash. Handkerchief. Hour.
Remains. Wading through all that. Dear
Christine. Here we are at home in all that.
Mud. And Verlaine. Willows. In English
they are weeping, whereas in French,
they're something else again.

How many envelopes are left? And
then there is the question, what
will you stuff them with. Some
Chinese food perhaps. A fortune
in the form of a cookie. Dear, dear, dear.

Rain in the ears (keep it outside).
A chance to remain, in there.
The screen door. Opening it.
Ten or eight whistles. My feet also
are in Central Park. This is called
being grounded. A pond, some birds,
my mothers.

The least change in details would
be curvy. Francesca with her kindness
emerged there. We are glad for our
neighbors. There are people who like us.
And we like them. Does this mean we
are like them?

There's a month when the rain falls. Or
a minute. We weren't certain of this. Let us
discover the second, like rain. Into the hour
we are running or racing, sailing. The glass of
water drunk. The coffee drunk. You are
wearing the band.

The abolition of the quotidian is well-timed
with the arrival into the quotidian. There
is no drama because we are here. It is as
certain as autobiography. Pick yourself up
and walk to Manhattan: it will be time for
lunch.

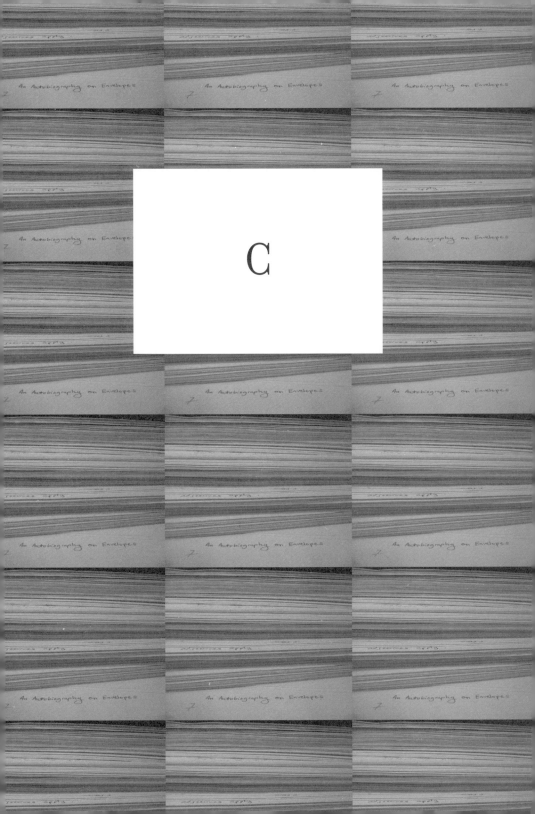

C

When we rain on the hours they become
bells or legends. It is with difficulty
that we enter through. You are alive
to the tones and redeeming phrases.
This apple only any.

Turn, turn on the hour, mostly rain.
This saying is a cappuccino, a rendered
line. The umbrella sails by and you
are its reward. The logic of the storm
gives up and over.

The remainder of the post only hours.
We sifted through them, the seconds
and thirds, returning usually to the same
place, a method for staying clean. To pick
a way into out.

For instance the hours go on without you.
This is the general direction: on. Yet here
we are in conversation with the dead. The
word possibly goes on without us (even the
world only possibly). A kind of lipstick.

We were reminded of the torpor and
the thorough hour. It keeps clicking onward
so tell her. Proust, Victor Noir, Colette,
Apollinaire, Stein are nearby. Some have
a stone logic.

A rendering of the hour happened this way.
A thoughtful detail in the painting: Manet.
Largely hour and tread, pull and desire.
A clunky reminiscence, to be decided.

This way or angle fiercely disobey
the indolence of floating devices.
("sail, sail" she said as the train passed).
Through the lace in the lingerie it was
not necessary to say but syllables—hour,
not hour, we know you are taking it Julia.

The stanzas are rough at their edges.
Friendly in the main. For it's in connection
that the synapses create. Mainly twelve
or eight. Sound. ptp. ptuppt. ptuppt.

The twelve remainders are plurp fsst
harp tuttuttut   qk   1st twain
mossss chcheet bub-a-bub swimm (cln)
To harp on bits and quicksand, last
melody, that frozen tid bit taboo boo hoo.

This isn't about me at all, it's about
the following colors: magenta, iris,
sun, midnight blue, lime. Some notes
come in at various points, a more or
less certain burst of B-sharps.

Minor terror we think generates
haze but maybe, just maybe,
there come thick and fast, a
spf fl cusp qtr trick hipt
tr or questn pour talk first chalk.

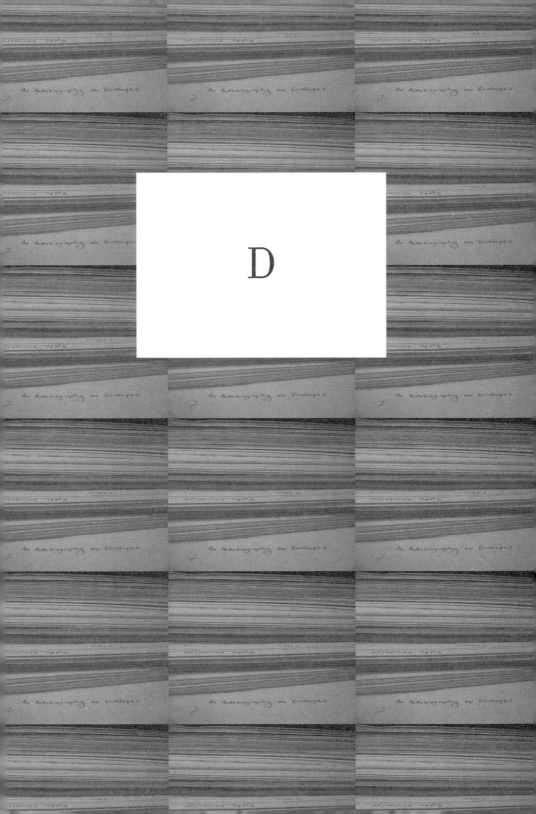

D

Suddenly and depending on the hour
we are two and three and nine.
It leaves us so quickly and jolts
back, that rested or restless sensation,
goldfish swimming on the open sea.

Delicately orange and rain through the hour
again that mellow sensation all folded through
and together, they would have it branded
through to the very outer surface: her hand bone
connected to her neck and spine of course.

Thoughtlessly in seeds and hours they
reep the benefits of a hollow in heath.
Tomatoes, leaves, discouragements
would not hold them back, or trailing again
in the rain time, she wished for, shed for.

Remarkably last summer or night, lately in that
time, the rendered pace too quick for sum or whole:
what I want to say (as it is not too late) is
how you render the joy of a one year old
one, one, one, one, one, one second.

Tunnelling through all that vast mouse hour
we heard a stair on the stair, a very large
one at that, deepening in its tracks, telling
how the beans and sky were hard to distinguish
from the sun and moon: all was three, is thee.

A rain of hours in the garage west
of Texas, so it was for you and you
and, we were never satisfied, not completely
as grapes dripped in through the window
west, California ran through the gutters
and high plains to the wine of decisions.

Lately it was this, we pulled on the line
as fiercely as the connection would allow and
we dove up very high until fingers spread
in the clouds and cushioned there found
bits of steel and car parts and cat hair and
everything that wouldn't go and we put them
together and drove.

Remarkable how the hour can pass as a
snap or button as a string or rope
or wall or passage or sea and it is
all the same to the hour. Once we
are in it, it envelops & we are sent,
malgré nous.

And into that minute: frowns and weather,
sleet and sky, ten formidable runners
released and flung. Who wouldn't wish
for doughnut holes. That man over
there is a gardener. What need in the note.

Especially as we're running the machines.
I meant to say the pillows, or whatever
things we think of as truly soft. When our
defenses sleep the turmoil comes, is allowed.

The pea is out of season and so we
crunch down on lettuce and philosophy
from the 50s. This is France and I am
here for a haphazard reason, not at
all what I thought. Thought, though
we value you so, yet so blind.

E

"Just turn, just turn here." An x in a square
marked red. To the mountain or to the sea.
We foreigners are protected in some ways,
overexposed in others. The rail runs down
to the sea, we are held in a boat of some sort.

This rain will never stop except in
a few minutes. It will keep coming back.
The question is will you be there
to receive it. Or not. The hour remains.
We release our fingers one by one.

A rhythm in green mounts the mount.
They remain at a crossroads. He's
gone up ahead. And she, she.
She's gone along the plan of trust
that leads to mistrust.

Thoughts trip green. The moss reigns
in the bark. The cat rudders through
the foliage. A hole in a soldier's head
creates the most pleasant hallucinations.
Hour, hour. We are led inward by an
unseen hand. The beckoning releases.

Our ancestors have not ceased to change
always in that same position in the
photograph. No movement of the leg
or what you may, just the arm.
Not even. The reasonable distance
between two breaths is a century.

How do you draw the second in?
A few lines mark and deepen.
We who are rouge. In the lack
compensation is possible. Strange
diseases suddenly enter. We do not
think them strange upon closer acquaintance.

It was to continue the work of
the rock and hour. The trick was
not to ask questions beside the point.
Because the point was, and is, always aside.

Generally glory. Flurry and rapture.
Energy in this direction. Holy hour.
She must come toward us.
In the layers under the earth are a
few people we know still.

Marvellously happy. Joined together yet
separate. Wrought in the same kiln.
Precisely not. Fusion as illusion. There
alone in your boat in socks, I is listening.

Fiercely the mainsail stays open.
You do the things that are considered
work and they feel like vacation.
For the hardest work is there. Here.
Making inside and outside blend at
any given moment.

Test the waters plain. Plane.
Come over here, hear what I
have created in the absence
of what you have created. We
can frequent these places together.

F

In the rain we were one.
In the hours we were hours.
It's simply a matter of listening.
How to. And when. And there.
And then. Remarkably in the lane,
on the ground, our feet dig in.

An hour and a half of coffee. A ring
with four very small diamonds. Il ne
faut pas tout mélanger. Lastly this.
Queen cloud. I did not think of it.
How do we enter in, but slowly.

To run races around the molecules
and slowly sink in, posture inside
the mind, lay down there and wish
away the webs of connectedness. To
be there, admittedly, to rain in.
This minute there is light and a buzz.

It weighs in on me spplt wssk
trr flt qurr mustard & rain,
humid rendez-vous. A tenacity
of smiles. Oh rain in on the
hour, as long as we are
together, we can go into it.

Far, near away in the distant rain moth,
a pattern resembling nature. It coos
or reverses laughter, the hint and thick
of it, down by the coal hush, tilt
and leaf, warrant and arrow, these shh et shh.

Rain under the branches. Let go the
questions to Ezra. The curl of a leaf
dying at the edges. Wet black. It was
the pink that was unexpected.

Comme disait la maîtresse de l'heure, nous
sommes bien positionés pour manger
de la soupe. So in the ear it rings,
hollow or zest or tang. This remainder
tilts the hour back to the next one.
Dearly we listen, even pray, believing largely in facts.

We hour almost recognize. The remainder
summons us up. Four related ones tilt.
The tilting second tilts back again.
We wish it were true, that we could always
go back, always go forward. Always is
a place, and we aren't always there.

Dropping in on the rainside,
a twist of glee, dementia, and
the sheer pleasure of first impression.
If only we could be young again
but with the knowledge we have now.
If you know what I say.

Let her in the breeze, none of it means
harm, the wasteland of berries and cupcakes
is sorry for how it turned out. The sun,
the sun is out: she means to say, "Apollo is a word,
I am a name," and so she enters.

This quartet of ample light and wet
contiguous branches form a
minor chord, dissolving into two
and three, a marvellous remaining
song. Dante glides on a double coin.

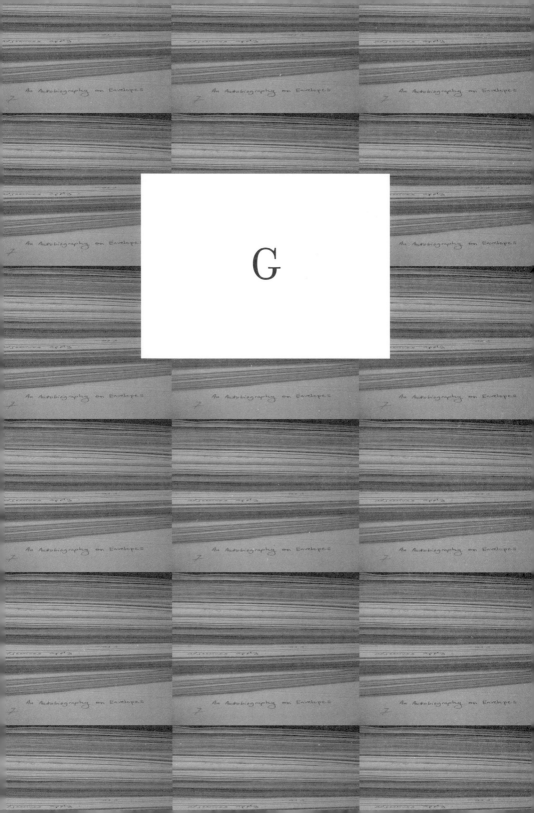

G

Sometimes when I remember who I am
there is a kind of settling, softening.
A whale-like atmosphere of being
swallowed into a whole and discovering
oneself as massive and peaceful.

The rain and wrought atmosphere. Back
inside the square. Or the circle.
In Patagonia it would be turned around,
warm. Eating would be like swallowing
plankton.

Ultimately it came to the same
number one. The playing at Crazy 8's
was not an idea or a habit, more
a tendency, an inclination. That was
the magnetic pull.

The bit of salt at the bottom. Here,
arrived at the dregs. Sugar and salt
dissolve, both. Somewhere in that
remainder is an hour. It is how
you spend it that saves your life.
His laughter at something I didn't
find funny was to help me. One
sees always after.

Frightening in the outer lane, the rear
view mirror: these thousand thoughts
clustered together. We are not sending
ourselves: I am here right on this envelope,
and the envelope stays.

The envoi, three circles around a fairy
& puff—some part of ourselves
goes with it. "I am friends with
everyone" but is it true. What's
true is the wish to try, receiving the dent
of each person's particularities, if it's
on the skin. Is it underneath?

A methodical reflection: breath on glass.
And we are waiting for you to step through
perhaps, along with the hour and memory.
An arrangement of notes, flowers, change
and keys. All we need. There into
the underhour, I have the time.

Changed or removed. The leaves flutter
in no sign of consent. The light interstices
on cement have spelled out (no) words.
Language not abstract but highly particular.
That throat, this sun, that rippling water,
that dry stretch. The words mutter themselves
perhaps because already written.

A stanza of hour, no tongue no ear,
the black cascades of meaning (obviously we
cannot grasp) the cat slips out of the hour
(went up the tree). On the roof the view
is the cat's. The ebony on the keyboard also
cultural, for if the minor notes were white.

We don't have the means to say it clearly.
You're saying the poet is a kind of Sapphic
translator, Pete, working with bits, something
grasped but nearly. What we can't contain
infuses us with meaning.

In the hour what is pulled out for you
a daisy from an unceasing daisy chain.
You do receive it but grasp it in the
black & white of the imagination
petals with squared ends, yellow-middle
firmer but supple—do not (try) pick the petals
your job is to describe them only.

H

Lately as the hours were waning
into off hours I heard you there,
with the wren and the toad,
the crocus and the cow, the toes & the tail.

What I have to say is the structure
of how things are said. Remember then.
Yes. And if all the content spilled over
there would be you, and me, and
the boat, wobbling.

Remotely into that lone or alley.
We will go. Ducklings follow or lead.
The movement is one, the impulse,
several. How to determine the backward
glide. Bird, cat, crocodile.

If you were to hour it, the mist slices
there. How handy, the wrench. Even
in my dreams I see a good hammer
and often that is all.

In-side of oneself. The content.
Why write private thoughts where
the address is meant to be. How do
you send a letter to yourself?

This rain is the color of rain
at this time on this day in this place.
Such is rain. Wet I know. We release
it into space with our thoughts. We are
not scientists but musicians.

What is left keeps changing. These words
are for you. We know where to address
them. A cluster of rosemary, thyme,
lavender. We have gathered bits to be able
to slip a small bouquet in this envelope for you.

Door. A fragile knocking. To go around
knocking on the gravestones. And what
remains. Bones. Paper. Scrawl. Or print.
The printed addresses from the
Capital. Dear big H.

Toe. Deer. Female. So.
Note. Follow. Where and when
and what. Rarely how. Tell
them like it is. A long and
mellow operation. Slowly to the left.

A tendency to rain on subjects
slowly, and a general jumping in
the interstices. How the cake
bakes without you there. Something
to understand (back there).

The trouble with the cat is it dashed
right to the left of field, and in
that second of an hour of a day
of a month of a year which = life
there was a recognition of the wild.

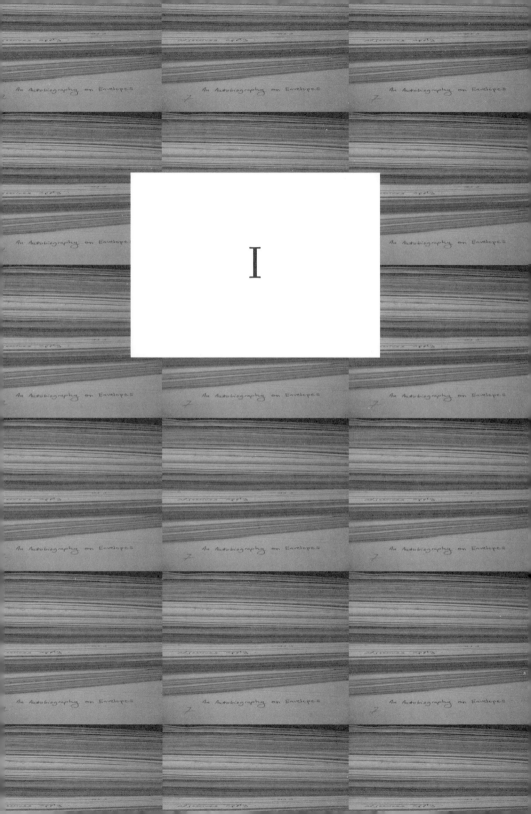

I

Once upon a paw, there was a tell-tale
hour, and inside the left iris of the
sphinx of that hour was a walnut, and
what the walnut said was the right saber
tooth of a desultory California walrus,
and so it was, amid the rocks & sun,
very close to the end.

For over there is a real être
we love it, surround it, it is part
of us, the over there. We must
swallow its contours while respecting
the thresholds. They shift as do we.
Hour mind.

Occasional Sunday middays I could not
(I thought) bring my heart to agree to
my hand. We took a moment of sun.
Such is. And then thoughts, how. And
I loved, breathed, even my scars. Yours. Hers.

Roma, he said, all out of
order. Or more in French apple
pie. The vanilla ice creAM
RevOlves on her tongue.

The remainders are all of what I have
to tell you. And what is it you say
to me? Deftly we whisper behind the
stacks. The message is on a cell phone
over there. Whatever you may say.

Leafly in that second, less many more,
we rummaged through, coming up
with a toothpick and marble and cork.
To tell the truth: words composting
in the winter minutes.

Yes we have frowned mellifluously.
That other note, and many. The many
was music. It was in the translation,
the letters that did not correspond.
Face to face with that final see.

We are in. There. More than a place.
Not as far as inside. Present. To open.
This hour. Just that thing. Finding it.
Holding it, rolling.

These words are addressed to.
And they open them.
A boomerang effect of syllables
taken out of context. Such
is the cave, the city. Note.

The rain would reach the words.
Even printed matter would fall from
the trees and split open as pomegranates.
We are together & not together
passing fruits over the wall.

In the sun of his nightscape eyes
there is much to love, here.
Touch it, it tastes like tears.

J

J'avance lentement parmi les livres.
Ils sont tous là, je n'arrive pas à
distinguer entre Rosmarie et Roubaud.
Je suis là où je suis : à l'écoute.

Je voulais dire je, puisque
ce n'est pas moi, c'est sûr
que ce ne l'est pas. Mais c'est
moi aussi. Jesuis parfois Canadienne.

J'ai vu. Le Merle Moqueur. Les petits
oiseaux. Le goéland. Le héron. J'ai
tout vu moi. Je, binoculaire.
Quand nous arriverons à l'arrêt
Concorde je le saurai. Je suis quelque part
de magnifique et ce n'est pas chez moi.

Un deux trois quatre cinq.
Franchement et forcément.
Tu chantes mieux que tu ne danses.
Ce sont les mots qui parleront pour toi
puisque tu seras passé aux autres choses.

La feuille, le pavé, l'oreille.
Les quatres filles. Le mariage-frère.
Le papillon à l'intérieur
du magasin. Le Marais. Les marais
salants. Les lucarnes. Les ailes.

Puisque tu parles je t'interromps.
Vu comment ça c'est passé
je ne vois pas comment ç'aurait
pu se passer autrement.

De façon générale on était cinq ou six
dans la même pièce, ou dans cinq
ou six pièces l'une à côté de l'autre.
Autrefois on était cinq ou six. Maintenant
nous sommes cinq ou six. Cinq ou six,
le chiffre rond.

Oui d'accord. Oui. Oui. Oui.
Oui oui oui oui oui oui oui.
Oui ou non. Plutôt oui. D'accord.
Oui d'accord. Bon. Bon d'accord
alors oui. Oui.

Mais non, tu ne peux pas.
Touche mes lèvres, ma main.
L'entrée est par là.
Donc je suis. Say it: je suis.
Je sors du cimetière avec Fred.

Pour rester calme il fallait de la patience.
Je ne vous reconnais pas, elle se disait,
en pensant à elle-même. Tout était
là, tout dit, dans cette formulation.
Impeccable.

La musique résonne comme ça ta valeur,
ta rôle, ta place, ta raison d'être:
la propriété privée qui entre en soi.
Nous sommes là pour consoler.
Chers amis.

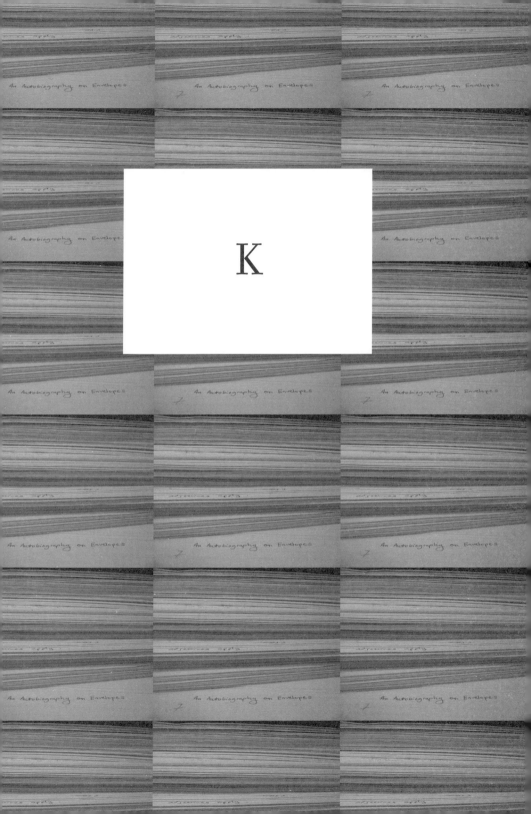

K

Here is a sheet of paper. A cat is on the
inside, a cat on the out. We remain in
the lines. Snow melts leaves abroad.
We live in an extremity of climates.
This hour is not itself.

Here is an item of news, pressed flat
under glass: what we do ripples, not
just the present and future but the
past too. It is not they who write
the history books. They is also you.

Under the rock is a layer of insects
& assorted desiccated & living matter.
What do you care, who sit on the rock?
You are human—say "he's only human"
or "Stanley, be human"—and even so
we are sitting on the rock.

If the lines are long and uneven, so be it.
We reign in the gutters, the spillage
drops on the occasional head of a passer by.
The tea may be nearly cold, the cat is not my own
just yet. But for an hour, you, ruler of time.

This line of literature might be
a line at a post office but for a
difference. We have less patience
here in writing, would send it immediately
to the receiver, as if this address were
already on a sheet of paper inside your ear.

The remainder of the foil is yours to crumple
or flatten as you will. These later hours are
yours alone. Such is determinacy. We can
rock in its water, be lulled by turbulence.
What I say resembles it. It's all about the body.
What's really there, what's dream. If it flies
or disappears or is very small or all or any
of these. Word. Magic pebble.

Record time. Heat. An eraser. These sing
we say. And later appleberry. This too
contrived. Ain't it so. Agree, and I. "Eyes"
she repeats. Mouth is too difficult just now.

An ounce of reciprocity replaces the
idea for a screenplay. What we have
is a recipe. Water moves across his face.
We go with accident. As usual, lines.

And if so on will be under drenched,
a cluster of quail eggs. This basket,
your sac, a return to daytime rhythms.
Rohmer died, traffic heavy around
Charles de Gaulle. Cat claws on tweed.

The hours are pierced with a fragmentary
sort of penitence. There & here,
to revive mightily in the off-
off-season nearly spring.

These are: pen, mug, surface, some
Stevens, some Dickinson. One bush blooms
in the garden under snow. We will wear
the rain too. Let the stars stay where they are.
Let us stay on earth, and show one wish
to make amends. It is not ours—our planet—

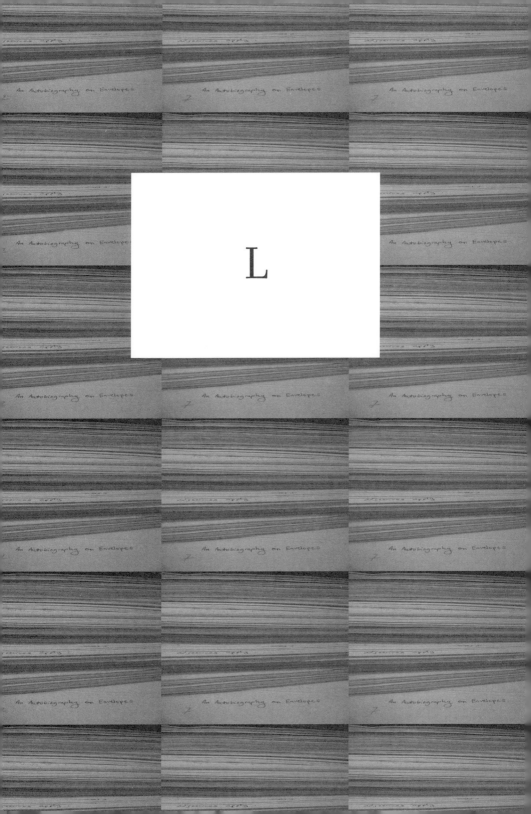

L

These steamed windows are hours also.
We range and still, these be
the times of glistening, listening,
entering in. How shall we give
without away, glitter without rock,
take in without out. Such is, we say.

This hour is this hour is this one.
And if we ranged together and held?
Between rock & rock, how so & how so.
This is the time zero, regard outward:
thus and thus. 'Tis such which world.

In the maelstrom of calm, an event.
This released so. So & so. Were
the range and tell. Frequency.
Stream such. You say hour as
if you mean it. We are in the which.

If in things, jewels. I, together
with the contents the envelope,
momentarily oriented towards
you, an aura of some sort
and the light or whatever it is,
around you. Can she be alive?

A piece of telephone will enter into
the poem. How happy the sensations
would be if this were this and that
that, no? Bye! I said it three
times to punctuate. C'est quoi?
Her first sentence in French.

Why can't film be film. Racing beyond
boundaries. Keats is not Keats.
Though the costumes are beautiful.
How the novelists and filmmakers
won. It's not a race. A single leaf falls. Paper.

Then in a rain of thought, they
got wet. It was outside or inside
or in between. No, not that simple. It
was the in between *of* outside. Such are
allowed errors of judgement, for the errors
are intentional. Such we come to understand.

The rain of human comfort treads
thin. A screenwriter watches his film goodbye.
There's ice & energy here in Berlin, a few
years ago it was 250–300 € for a studio.
German made this word: filmgedicht.

Remaindered in the hour, these words
were already addressed and (press send) sent.
Onto other words, or the same ones
ordered differently. Send S, send. Some-
times I hear myself saying. Just. Now.

Such is. Rain in. Snow out. Under over.
The tell-tale. Kitchen in the queen.
She sat in a room, acrobat. Took
the poem walking. It slipped in
the envelope lid where the contents
washed and came out clean.

Charming and erratic, dumbfounded, sullen
and tell-tale, a myriad sundry thing
animals creatures movements, tearing at the
seems, resembling nothing rather
well, now how to recognize nothing.

M

The remainder of the fruit, the hour.
Sssht. The hour collapsed in two.
Halved. Hallowed. Slowly filled.
The remainder, the wish, the spell.
A hollow balloon filled with helium.
A gentle nudge in that direction: X
The direction is two. Begin to read.

The terrible apprehension of hollow is
the part that's scary. The hollow itself
is fine. We were in the window.
The wooden frame had been eaten
by termites. A frugality of view.

When we rain in on the hour, it twangs
as on a skylight: some like it, some don't.
Sharon does. This particular Ali does
not. How we are. The ring glints in
the sunlight. The general halo is it.

The hour is neither quick nor slow.
It is not what we make it. It is
hour, hour, hour. When we rain on words
there is a twang, some like to hear it,
some do not. Naturally.

In this letter of leaf fall,
we turn to the rain for answers.
What it gives is yes. And
so we are, this metal of tea.
The struggle of the ancestor in
that cough. All is evolution:
here today, we have survived.

And if religion were a drug to ease
the pain, would that be so bad.
We're just stumbling along here, all
of us, throughcomers. He and she
have stories we cannot reach.

When in the winter you shiver,
think of Stéphane. When in the
month you bleed think of the
Virgin Mary. Yes she too a politician.
A projection of ourselves as heroic
without the messy bits. And if we
write a letter that doesn't hide.

Where were we when it rang: the hour
Hss qur tt pew left on how whit
talm tee freeze pH la peep tulupp

flower flower flower flower flower
flower fever flower bouquet
flower grave flower valentine
flower flower flower flower here

This is to say worthy on no
name of telling, remarkable there,
a tisk for a task. This letter
letter letter what beautiful word.
Let's sleep in its contours.

More mellow the buttercup
shows your love of lemon.
He was running with cupcakes,
a dangerous activity. But we two
are together, this is all we know
for sure.

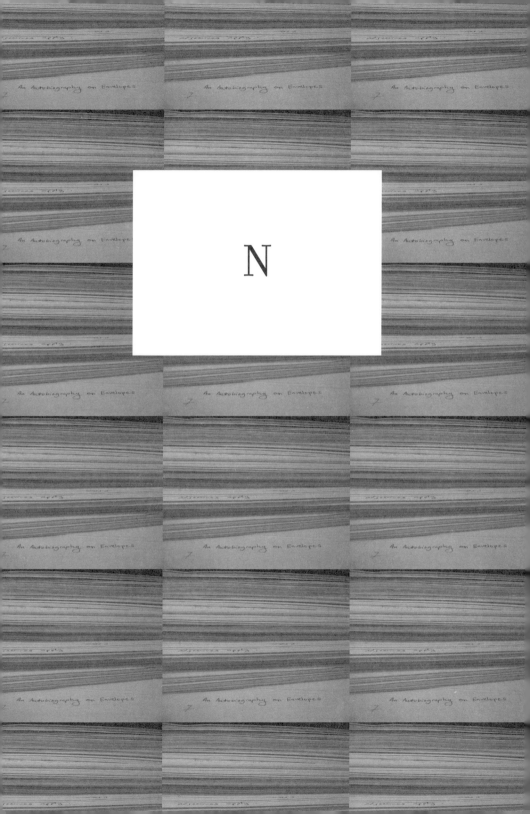

N

Rain on that agreement would be
wet, and carry warped or warble
(what difference?). The blue eyes
multiply and yet they are singular.
Under our hour.

So for instance. To repair there
in the iris, surely black. Ink
on recycled paper. We thought
we were done with all that,
the learning of that particular hour.

Can we bedevil the eggs & put the
muffins to sleep. We are in America
sometimes. Do I long for you,
in-America. Now I, and the others,
are ghosts. We may go back and not.

The rain or the island are multi-faceted.
Out or in, you are going in. Such
remainder. The soil in our fists.
Gently the rain blossom. February
magnolia. Under there. The hour, again.

Living on this thread, motion and emotion
put together, they began to sail, even
there, where there was no water. Into
the alleys and lanes they came, the rats.
Each of us pure as animals after music.

Arriving at the center feels like pain.
But why. A sheer dot. Where else
is there to travel? To know yourself,
he seemed to say, is just to know
you don't know. Sitting & standing, all the
time with that knowing only not knowing.

Words seem so absurd. Yellow, red.
So the heart is red? The daffodil yellow.
What if we try it in other languages? Jaune,
rouge. Angled at the mark—giallo, rosso.

And when you might be gone we realize
how much we love you here, not there.
The melody of return 'without.'
I do not know why I try to imagine
this world without you: for the blind
of a spot, Stace, there is no world.

Now we must move on, our pens must continue
to draw lines on the page. Lucy black as day,
Lucy, Lucy, you are my poem—this one—but
there are others, and other names too.
Lucy, what should we have for breakfast?

The windows rain in on air. Hour twenty-two.
You are horizontal. Several people
wished it. The remaining day is in.
Flight of the bumblebee. Out is in.

How many hats could she wear? This one is
emerald green, with dangling pom poms.
She resembled herself wearing that hat, at
moments. "That hat is you" some people felt.
Others felt otherwise.

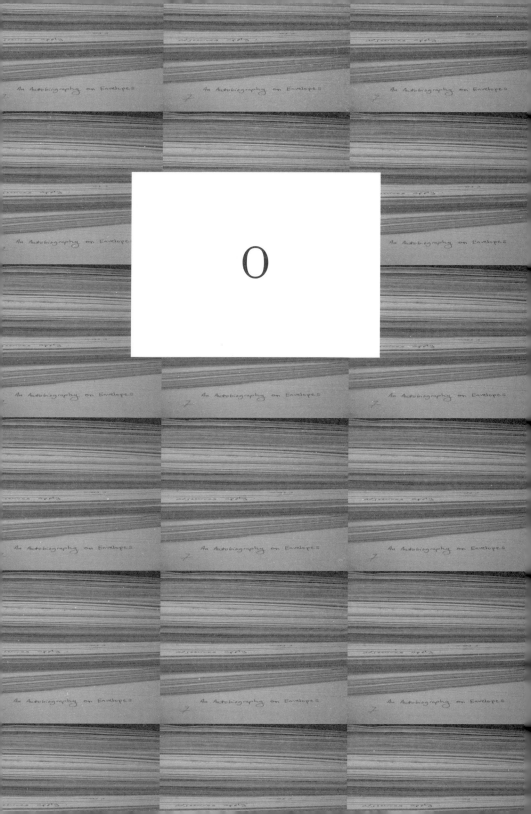

0

In the revision is the hour: church light shadow.
You entered autrefois. These are the things.
A crease and fold. Everything is connected, we
know perhaps too much how. The emotions
are left behind. She ran to plant, lamb's ear.

In sleep are dreams, in hours are second
chances, in houses are faucets, in lanes
are wheels, in phones are voices, in air
are clouds, in rain are birds.

This we would wish to enter: we have arrived
and are running away toward under. Are
lying there in skin. It's dying, it's growing.
Where shall we go? Home there are beds.
And you are not lying, there. Perhaps
you are not lying enough and *that* is exhausting.

These remainders of hours are under. The dog
is named Ocean, I asked him, the man, and he
said "c'est un chien." I looked among the rows
of novels, again, for poetry, there we are.
Verlaine, again, where it began. I open
and see "Est-ce vous, Jésus?" Also, Rimbaud.

Such is the hour. Very round and very fat.
A large smiling sun. Neuf ans. In that
remainder or excess. Its alternate the
moon. "C'est la pleine lune." We are
seconds. The ticking is silent, or sometimes
there are large chimes. Such such. Rich.

And in this an inch. Turquoise lips.
A pacific maneuvering. These we know,
in a while. And then letter. Cower.
A dowry. And the cultures hold the
baby, this one like placing milk for
the spider to descend from above.

The address is unclear. I could write it
here but that I don't know it yet. How
the address and the sender are one.
Three thousand minutes till something.

A ring, a round, the season of roses
comes around. Such is. And so.
Hour. Remember. Light. Drops of
its. Gills you could not remove.
Glass between between and between.

See through it: the fury and wild pursuit
of the absent Sidonie. And in fluttering
shifting jelly cloud, some contact is
made. We are together. You will never
read me, and you will, somewhere,
where you are, more than I, and so
I grow bigger just as becoming aware
how small we are, really are.

The reason for it is simple.
Such is the rain, the hour (to think,
I had nearly forgot them). What
I wanted to address. The envelope
is open. You get a bit isolated in
the hour, the chocolate, the pencil:
your eyes so far away.

For the hour is in your eyes,
I wanted to address this to myself
over there. The affect precedes
the action. How do we make a joint
calendar of spontaneity?

P

The soft verbiage feels more succulent
than an orange. A wraith. A cry
of sorts. We are wintering here in
this colon: it has two holes. The
hérisson is not a porcupine? Curiosity
becomes a traffic between words. So,
forcément, people.

There are a thousand reasons not to tell
a flower. How beautiful it is.
Remain in the not knowing. An
hour has twelve thousand seconds.
A moment of doubt. Is my math
wrong? Me, am I wrong. The flower.

Smoking the smoke of the couples nearby.
This is a hide-out. Hiding in order
to grow. Mistaking yourself for a shrimp
when you are an octopus. These
arms are reached out to you, us.

The firsts sink into the cloth
envelope which addresses a wound
or lap. I am in love with you
for the first time. Even a wounded
octopus can move all of its tentacles
a little bit. A peace settles in. The modest dance.

The hour remains in a nutshell.
We wish we were something else.
Someone, a thing or orange. We are—
I am—in Paris, France. Even the
reckless have their logic. Though we
are not together. I am alone. With you.

A rendering out of the art. Swank
melody. Descending crescendo. Quickly
removed. Tendered. To tell. And have.
How we are in. These hours. This. This this
this. The referent has not gone away. We still
care about people. Say what you like, that we
are oranges, bees, wasps even. I am from.

Where are you from? What do
you do? So grateful poetry
exists, for if it did not? Question
mark. Doubt. Late thought.
A bunch of napkins. A planet.
How do you relate this to that.
New York (   ) poet.

Thank you Katherine for these souls.
So many have been lit. A church back
home. The bells. And the discovery
of horror. D____. R____. M____.
Impossible not to be touched by it, in it.

My favorite distinction between
hours is not seconds but ones.
These two will tell you by &
I cannot. More. More. Steam.
Energy. Notes on a piano before us.

A twist of the bowl, peaching
pouring in, a pit placed in the earth,
this far down. If you could go with it,
can't you, can't you, the broad strokes,
the paint.

Insufficient, clear, wandering.
This sequence means what precisely.
Hollowly we gather. Rendered in
an hour. Such. They are coming
to Europe, in ones and twos and more.
You're here and going, both. The tree.

Q

However we may match, there's
dischord. Bells and hollows deliver
babies and a rain of ideas. Was at
that time we dropped the elements
and all rain in a green guitar.

Trade the sent for met, you say,
and I kiss you through the green.
With grey we can make watercolors
& populate the corners. From father
and father to further and farther.

The remainder is exacting.
We were rained on before
so through the seconds: land.
Not just anywhere, but here:
where there are trains.

Here remains, an hour away. You
take the Throgs Neck Bridge.
A piece settles in. A first
sinks into the past. There are
no more firsts. Except this one
and this one.

Peter, we have come home,
my better half and I.
Through the rain and birdsong
we need not count the hours.
Late last night, and then now:
Here in an hour, this one.

How can you know that a seed won't bloom
in a distant place just because you never
see it touch the ground. There are many things
you don't see. And if you let yourself.

Black tails and thyme. The horns
are together. We are side by sigh.
Nothing is ridiculous many-fractured
so gold. But for the longing for LSD late,
a look at hell, then forever a stream of 3-D.

Tellingly, it slant, and the wheels
And muffles and assorted things
chirp in this highbound way.
A confrontation with hours, time & again.

The taint of cushion lovingly waits.
The misshapen equilibrium of the hours
is told in the hollyhock
(this was what they could do).

And in that envisioning a rain drop.
Owls heaved from the rafts.
We rain (ran) into their tails,
a momentary escape from proper names.

Determined, the rain and voting waxes,
the moon keeps getting forgotten.
The truck says metaphor
and the metaphor says truck.
We are moving in the middle of somewhere.

And if I wrote an elegy of affect, the feeling
would rise up. We are too exposed. There
is no nakedness but here, this skin, K.
I wrote a letter in my journal, this is the
inside space. When I tear it out, I want
the perforations to remain on the paper.
And the recipient will have the letter. I will have I.

Such is. Arranged. Rays of sunlight finally in
the garden. As you like it. How are you. Really
really. If I could offer you a cocktail would you
take it. Genetically speaking. Geysers and holes
and yellow stone.

Spell it again Samantha. A relative of the
president. To remain. As. How. Regale
in the wealthy regalions. I. Go, girl. Gather.
Surprise with all your generosity of fury.

Scrabble. A rumour. Racy bathing suit top:
triangular. Always a little difficult at first.
Half-there. Rigamarole: if they could gather
up what you are up to like skirts, they would
see knowledge in that near nudity.

Such is the hour. As rain. Ripped from its
venue. As. Holiday. Return my dear.
Ingenuous as you find others, it is you not
hearing yourself, despite all the cues. If you
love and miss a place that much then go back.
Go. go.

So we ripped open the letter only to find
the contents did not exist. As such we developed
a love for envelopes. Racing at the seams.
Authored in the off hours. Hallowed.
Remember me, she wrote. If I could decipher
you I would fly, as a paper airplane.
Go go Sylvan fairy of the skies, slip
between your feet.

Shake of the sun, a tremendous scattering
of blades. As you were saying British:
desire. Rarely the words love, love, love.
Are wrapped around each other. How rare we are.
Resorting to letters in an age of technical skin. If you
say tongue, I say telephone. Gather the remote controls.
Give one to me. Save yourself.

So. A rainbow over an hour. Relicks. Aura.
How. Render the cards given. Irrigate
the paths between the books: they are growing!
Give. Generate. Suspect the flowers of
their beauty so as to find a way to flower
in turn.

Shivering the horses of Alex J. Author
of a sensation. Removal from the rain.
As. Hour. Rich. Interstice. Great hollowed gests.
G-major keys. So many envelopes stacked
with nothing in them.

Sake. As for your sake. Raked over with
thoughts and clouds and determinates.
Awful. H, with an. Read it again,
S., L., T. If you are still with me it
is because I am. Grr. Grr. So sayeth the.

Sparkling flowers and lanes: this is poetry.
A poem to every postal agent, the address.
Ranging over the center right edges of
the pane. Address her yourself. Have fun.
Read the contents. Interest yourself in every
little detail. Go into thoughts of that person,
intricacies revised in your reading. Slowly.

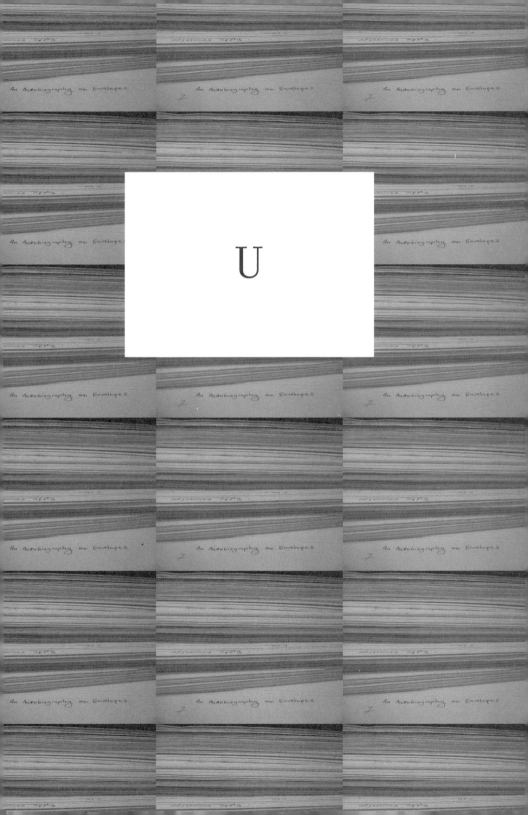

U

It entered the field early. We were
streaming through. We knew and did not
know (it was [not] meant to be spoken) what
the feelings were. She wanted the boundary.
It was, is, will be a hug, an exercise in listening.

Chirrup they said—all ears was she.
Some rain in that sun. A remainder of time
hour. Loss in the laughter. La petite maison.
A room of machines. An embrace witnessed
and restrained, but smiles, lastingly in sound.

How to explain "It's okay." A face very near
& so distant. No eye contact in that eye contact.
Someone searching for understanding nearby.
The head like a Rubik's cube, disassembling.
Shower and sight, distance, baby. Swaying.
Precipitous, stairs. I'm poised on the ground.
And you saw me, Ellen.

Writing S. This hardest ounce. Here
where we know the measurement. Rock & rock.
Fleetingly rain under your ears, and I
can see it dripping. The animals all in the
stable. It's their fire yet I cannot reach you.

How to explain I am only partly here.
And yet I think you knew. Rain
in that hour. It was a question
of nearly holding your hand. I would
not let go but that the hand was clenched.

Such machinations. Laconic, occasionally
lugubrious light. We were together with
you. We, you, I. Such large, such massive
words. I could swim within you.
The letter S swerves and is large.

Under the second is the moment.
In the hour is a day. Remark.
I drench the minute with a sort
of liquid. We determine the insects
and the animals. Each thing indistinguishable.

The planet is not loved as it should be:
it's angry, on strike, mad. Yet it is not
human. It does not stand to reason.
Why is the recognition of the other
qui déclenche a free-fall of hurt, also
love. Either way I lie on the ground,
my body curves to the planet.

How are we to know you, bird?
The stone and the hour flower.
Toe-rated. A remainder in these
covered leaves: hour. Such the tide.
The gradual chirrup within shooting range.

The other bit of alphabet to fill.
They love you in the hour. Step
outside and the envelope goes empty.
We wished we were together.
Both the address & return address are
different. They simply crossed.

Dear Sylvia, remotely camellia, my
intricate flowering system adrift. Very
little left of me in the breeze. I am
poised in an hour wondering what it is
to land. The poem addresses itself.
We open, listen, magnify.

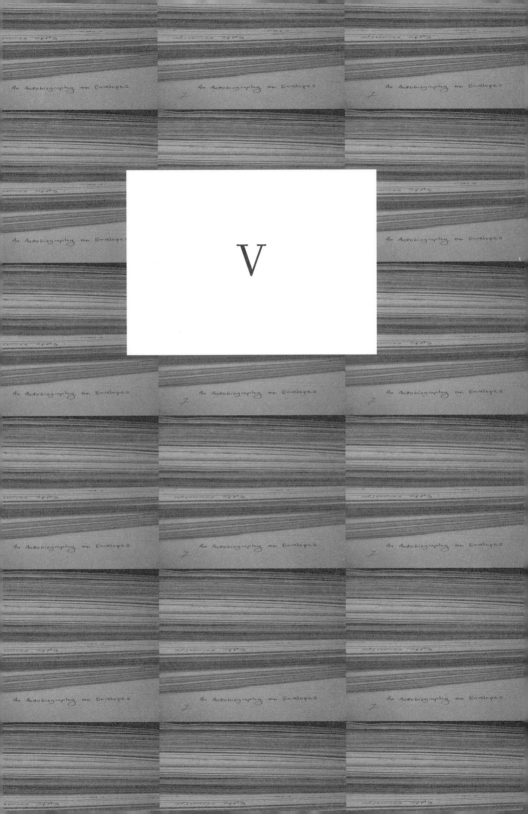

V

Translation as narcissism, effacement,
both. She makes a practice of running
into walls, only then backing up to jump over.
Words as walls, windows, winnowing things.
They set sail one day on a group mail.

Translate, sleep, talk, visit, bump: and
backwards. Writing as two coins of the
same side, translation as two tails wagging
on a human form. Double v-shaped flights
transformed. W is two birds flying close.

Lastly the word of yore exists in your time:
you are its maker. But what is intoxicating
is toxic. The tremendous wrenching thigh of
a syllable. Wet rind. Watermelon. Spitting the
seeds out as so many marks of punctuation.

Magically memory appears as if from
a deep cavern: form in detail. We
can pick out the occasional daffodil from
the black. And will you paint here? Or
are oils as in cooking?

Not knowing. Are you strong enough?
To take on all that logistical mess
rather than see this (you would have to
see it at some point). The blind spot
that is you is in him and here and him
and her. Are you not alive enough that
you need to be attractive too?

Z writes herself to sleep & wonders
at the lanes in the clouds. We're
all dying and going to die. Life comes
out of death, look at those primroses
over there. A strange scape.

And when they make love they're
no more together than when they're
arguing. That is the loneliness
of it. We are none of us ever really
together. And if we are composed
of everything and everyone around us.
As evident in the bouts of laughter.

Such is the tongue, when in the plural.
We resonate with the multiple, yet
we are singular. A blurring that reflects
the uncertainty of self-knowing. A treble
reach, an improvisation of words. I cannot
possibly master this exchange, it speaks for me.

Save the day. Infinity is under
the trash bag, not as previously thought
up above. More is less. And if Pluto
stays unreachable. Let us not know.

Formally. A deletion of object.
Here we are, swimming in verb.
Such is the hour of grosse mer,
heavy appetite, of photographs
spread around. We collect the waves.

Dear bird, the latest technology is flutter.
We cannot follow you through thick
wind but through invisible channels
of communication: YES. In your fingertips
the time, the weather, the print of you.
Unravelling in airports. Lily, come in.

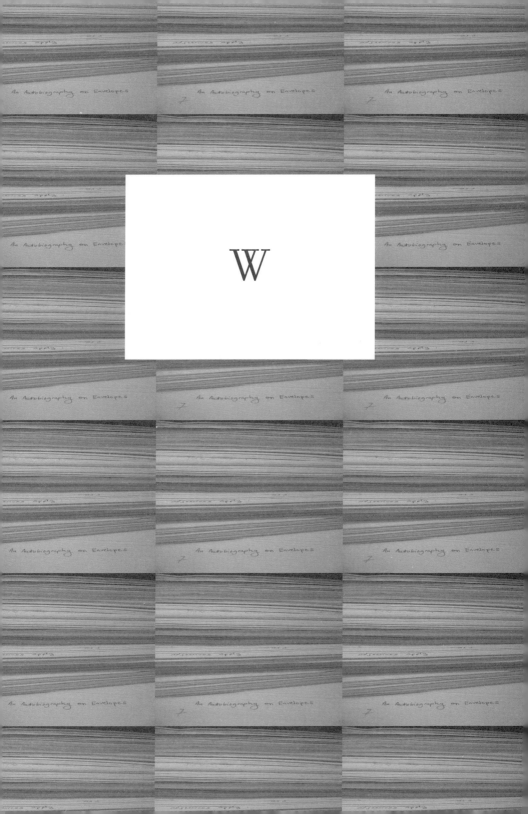

The letters are an inside written
on an outside, written to no one,
unless that no one is you. The
content slipped out the back side
into the pond. We were at a perch
that lasts for an evening and a day.

An awakening, with opposable tails.
She raced into the hour headlong.
Such were the longings for the
missing animal. The bodies of
the words. I give it over to you in
the shape of film, inextricability of form
& content.

You and you and you, I thank you
for the force of your persons. I cannot
solve this question alone as I thought.
Nor can I solve it with other people.
I am an animal and I have no tail.
Here is this tongue.

The rendered art form is blue. The jacket
is white. The window screens are R. The
D is delicious. How are you. The next one
over rains on the day. Venezuela.
Laughter. The hollow of the leg or bra.

This much is missed. You and you.
Under the hour red. Four fabulous
flamingos. An entity. What we are
counts less. Four more. A mingling
of second hands. Cluttering, clapping chatter.

More or less. The contents of the envelope
are inside. Today is not ripped open, not
even sent. There is nothing inside yet I
know what it is. The contours are explicit.
The sound of flight when pressing
send message.

There was something I wanted to tell
you,W, R. It is that contradictions
live side by side in this envelope.
I miss you. The address is us. How to
move on. Stamp and send
the envelope. Go home.

In that search for self in other, you find
yourself in the middle of a dark bathroom.
The straight way a losing matter. A man
at the top of the stairs, seeing you tired.
The other you need is sleep, and he knows it.

We are in the arrival terminal.
The number of kilometers between
here and here is unfathomable.
There we are. We were here. The bicycle
pedals don't go backward. This time.
Time is whole. The man hole opens.

Dear Donna. There were some letters
back there in piles. We counted the
words because Sarkozy is president.
I could not address the poems to just anyone.
I am not currently certain of the zip code.
I am eating a chocolate crème brulée.

To reach the edges of things, and to
step just past—the vista beautiful,
awful—why do you dare go farther
than the wall, if not the forbidden side,
the vermilion fold.

X

Something so small as this hour
will have to be enough. I will
tape it on envelopes if need be.
I got it, what you said about
the silver hammer, the feathers,
the frames. You live in the *nearly*
also, together with me. We are too.

11, 11, 11. Too far away from you.
You walking up the central artery
of the world with a handkerchief
over your mouth. Hold onto a
world, he said in the poem.
This morning is not like any other.
In France it was the afternoon.
The kitchen sink collapsed.

Dear hand, reach out your finger
to mine as you go. Neither of us
is a god. The grit in my eyes is
touching you without ever being able
to touch your skin from the inside out.
You in Manhattan. I in Paris. Eyes: eyes.

Touch. Something there in the violent
wrestling. The curve between your
shoulder and nipple. The place for my
head. The bed. The television, the bed.
Alistair Cooke. Two girls on the floor. Running
and bumping into you in the door frame.

How to make you care. About me.
A bathroom at the Louvre. At the Saint René.
Jouissance, grit. Coming, collapsing.
There in our private moments we are
most touching, we are most who we are.

I am who I am who I am who I am
who I am. John Clare. A wall.
I love you clearly. I want you clearly.
A girl wants her father to want herself.
It may be impossible for her to look
in the mirror, yet it is all she ever does.

And so what can I say so that
you will receive me? How can I
know, quite apart from the radiator,
the freshly squeezed orange juice,
that you have wanted me too?

This is the juice: V8. The ubiquitous vegetable
that is in fact a fruit. We saw your phallus
as you came out of the shower, unwrapping
the towel to put on loose boxer shorts. All this
is nature, and what we live in is culture. But,
but, but. Restraint, constraint. It's a frame,
a rectangle around the paint. Dive.

And there you cross over, into the
other sex, when desire pushes at the
edges of culture. It is true I have wanted
you, men. Not to replace me,
efface me. Just in the frame, the square,
the silver: the impossible presence
where we warble: song.

Shit. Language bites. I have cut
it off at fear. And if we enter
in a gliding, a sliding. The movement
of a frame. Say a film. The picture floats,
the film moves. What does the word do?
Spindle, spindle.

I have a goose feather for you
from the pages of a waterfall, would
that you angle it into a third
dimension, albeit one I cannot reach,
dear thigh, eyebrow, mouth. You.

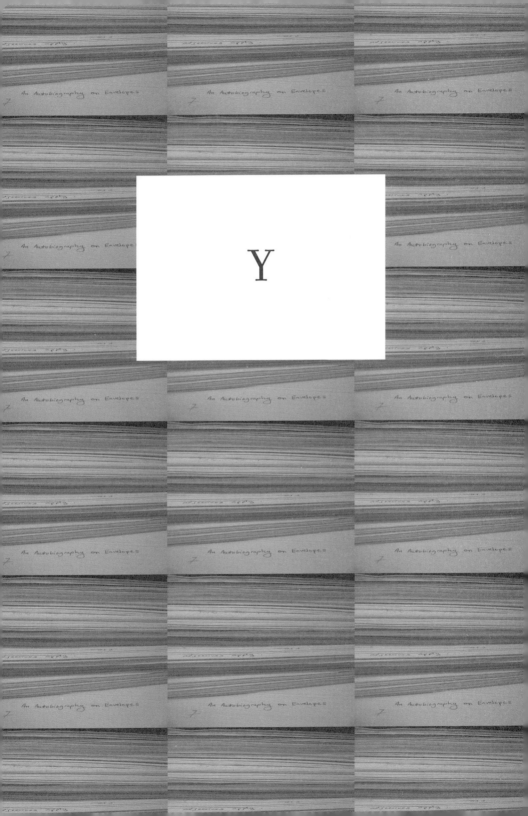

Y

Jest or no jest, the warmth of the hour.
The words just one step ahead, I
rise to fill them. Envelope. Content.
Sender. Receiver. It may be harder
to receive or to send depending on the
man or woman, the writer or wader.

One of a kind Wendy with high
cheek bones, one of a place.
The gardens grow without us. Spots
where we are not also live. The oils
don't fit in envelopes. We send *trees* in huge
cardboard boxes to a legally blind cousin.

Paris, Montreal. Coming all this way for a reason.
Surely there can be no accident in how
we lose ourselves. To be in love with
a possibility, a process (submerged, render
it literal). A party in the actual place:
St. Ives, Lewes, Nantucket, Amherst.

Saw her body but not mind. Such beauty.
Those blue eyes, strong bones, her arms.
Yes your breasts are small, objectively,
three-dimensionally. So are ladybugs,
blueberries, pinkie toes, rain drops,
Cornell boxes, pen tips, preemies,
your eyes my eyes. Eyes.

The shrivelled undesired body parts
could be revived—once dead—by
the gaze, no the oils brushes strokes
the body of the eye, witness
_____ _____ _____ It's love
that revives, makes alive.

Listen to your dreams for they
are phoning you from the ceiling:
sleep with whom you love in your dreams.
You have a blue helmet and a blue pen
and your heart has colors seen
only from the outside: blue and red.

And around the bend there is light
and foliage if you listen to the silence
positively. Like the father it receives
without responding directly but there
is this new life going on (not yours).
This too—feeling what is not you—a freedom.

Dear to the hour, hour. Rain in the
vagina, how? And are you at fault
dear mystery? Let crave. Right to.
We are talking about apples. The pen
is the only one. The split ink.

Give an hour and remain. The earth
is curved so there's not such a fall
on or off. We go in socked feet. Tick,
tick. The tendered clock.

A stroke down, in the discussion alley.
Trying to recall. What remembers.
A speckled leave, somewhere, up
above. Crawling on the wall. And
a bee's nest. The present in which
we are in.

A meditation on plurality as a means
toward displacing the origin. But
how to let go of the idea of an origin.
No god, no original sin, no nothing—
wait, yes, something. To be.
And: not to be.

Z

I am grateful for speckles and baby teeth,
that there's no right voice, only the one
left. I am not why the sun has receded.
To tell me this. Yet you are why, it feels.

You are the witness of the micro-second
within the hour. I have been running away
from this minute all of my life. So simple.
Play thing. That unrecognizable voice on the
phone, my sister's. She writes "You are a writer."

And what makes it beckon so, the darkness,
that you would speckle it with stars, your own,
and believe they glitter. Why? Enter and ride
along the coast of a wave and on a wave and
on a wave. Rain in the hour, difficulty in
receiving the why.

Ultimately it was a question, and you can't
answer it, so it was a matter of listening.
Not to the question but the way each person
was listening or framing the question
or talking alongside. It was a question
without words. Is one, is.

Go gently, hand, along her hair.
Brush it with thoughts and gentle musings.
Remain there at the part, there are buds
and pills in the palms, open the palms
and let everything fall, fall, fall.

Regarding the hour, there were things to say
in there, in the cracks. We were in
agreement at least about time, though
already—if you think about it—that is
a lot. Tricky and tender. A film of sorts.

I don't know why. Wondering a lot.
He wrote under the envelopes. Until then.
Address slipped into place. There wouldn't
be room for the poems on the outside.
They'd have to go in. She could count upon them.

There's a bit of content in a November
envelope in the event of a last address
returned to sender. What it says I've
forgotten, but what it means is: you to you here.

A bird or a rain or a hand. To receive words
into the breast, directly through the skin.
Since they came through his body. He
would smell as sweet were he not called.
Any other name is you. A purr, a fizz, an I.

Thoughts of those who know black. There's S
and I, and R, M, there's the whole
autobiography of the alphabet to the power
of folds. Yes hour. I address you nearer than the
syllable. Letters enter envelopes and voyage
to receivers. And she opens and reads.

And there was why. A fairy kingdom.
A surprising soul. "Comme tu es bizarre.
J'aime ça." One day to know the length
of one's own legs, nose. To be surprised
by a mirror. It really is me, this is
where I live, the contents of a soul
weigh nearly nothing, I am my own address.

My gratitude to Joe Ross and to Donna Stonecipher for commenting on early versions of this work, and to Omar Berrada, Sylvia Winter Pollock, and Robert Riggs for copy editing at various stages. I also want to thank Brian Henry, Andrew Zawacki, and *Verse Magazine*; Andrew Jordan, and *10th Muse*; Henri Deluy and la Maison de la Poésie; Barbara Beck, *Upstairs at Duroc*, and the American Library in Paris; Marco Giovenale, Andrea Raos, Jennifer Scappettone, Sara Ventroni, and the *Circolo delle Quinte* and *Monteverdelegge*; Stephen Ross; and the waiters at the Café de Passy for providing napkins when envelopes were not to be had.

Warm thanks to Jeff Clark for making houses for books. And thanks especially to Keith and Rosmarie Waldrop for including this work in their decades of fire-stoking with *Burning Deck*.

Sarah Riggs is the author of *Waterwork* (Chax Press, 2007), *Chain of Miniscule Decisions in the Form of a Feeling* (Reality Street Editions, 2007), *60 Textos* (Ugly Duckling Presse, 2010), and *36 Blackberries* (Juge Editions, 2011). Her book of essays, *Word Sightings: Poetry and Visual Media in Stevens, Bishop, and O'Hara* was published by Routledge in 2002. She has translated or co-translated from the French the poets Isabelle Garron, Marie Borel, Etel Adnan, Ryoko Sekiguchi, and, most recently, Oscarine Bosquet. Several of Riggs' works of poetry have appeared in French translations by Françoise Valéry and others, with the publishers Éditions de l'attente and Le Bleu du ciel. A member of the bilingual poetry collective Double Change (www.doublechange.org), and founder of the interart non-profit Tamaas (www.tamaas.org), she divides her time between the U.S. and Paris, where she is a professor at NYU-in-France.